THE GREAT PYRAMID
OF GIZA

Measuring Length, Area, Volume, and Angles

Janey Levy

PowerMath™

The Rosen Publishing Group's
PowerKids Press™
New York

Published in 2007 by The Rosen Publishing Group, Inc.
29 East 21st Street, New York, NY 10010

Book Design: Daniel Hosek

Photo Credits: Cover, p. 30 © Roger Ressmeyer/Corbis; p. 5 (Snefru's pyramid) © Yann Arthus-Bertrand/Corbis;
p. 5 (Step Pyramid inset) © J. G. Edmanson/International Stock; p. 7 © Peter M. Wilson/Corbis; p. 9
© Roger Wood/Corbis; p. 13 © Will & Deni McIntyre/Corbis; p. 17 © Jeremy Horner/Corbis; p. 21 © Gianni
Dagli Orti/Corbis; pp. 25 (chest and throne), 27 © Sandro Vannini/Corbis; p. 25 (king's fan) © Archivo
Iconografico, S.A./Corbis; p. 28 © Gian Berto Vanni/Corbis.

Library of Congress Cataloging-in-Publication Data

Levy, Janey.
  The Great Pyramid of Giza : measuring length, area, volume, and angles / Janey Levy.
      p. cm. — (Math for the real world)
  Includes index.
  ISBN 1-4042-3353-9 (library binding)
  ISBN 1-4042-6059-5 (pbk.)
  6-pack ISBN 1-4042-6060-9
  1. Mensuration—Juvenile literature. 2. Great Pyramid (Egypt)—Measurement—Juvenile literature. I. Title. II.
Series.

QA465.L48 2006
516'.15—dc22

                                                    2005014919

Manufactured in the United States of America

Contents

Ancient Egypt, Land of Pyramids

When you think of Egypt, you probably think of the most famous Egyptian monuments—the pyramids. The pyramids were created by the ancient Egyptian civilization, which began about 5,000 years ago.

The pyramids were built to serve in the **afterlife.** Ancient Egyptians believed that each person had a spirit, or *ka,* that lived on after the person died. A person's most important task during their lifetime was to prepare for life after death. Rulers and wealthy people built tombs to be homes for their *kas.* The earliest tombs were simple structures that resembled large benches. Then, around 2750 B.C., King Zoser (ZOH-suhr) built the first pyramid. It was not a true pyramid. It looked like giant steps, so it became known as the Step Pyramid. King Snefru (SNEF-roo) built the first true pyramid about 150 years later.

The ancient pyramids are engineering marvels. We still don't know exactly how they were built. We do know that their construction required impressive knowledge of math. We can learn more about the pyramids and the people who built them by using our math skills to study the most famous Egyptian pyramid—the Great Pyramid.

Step Pyramid

pyramid of Snefru

The Step Pyramid, shown in the small picture above, is about 200 feet (61 m) tall. That's about the same height as a 20-story building. Snefru's pyramid is about 345 feet (105 m) tall. That's almost as tall as a 35-story building!

The Great Pyramid of Giza

The Great Pyramid is the largest of the pyramids that rise above the Giza plateau, less than 5 miles (8 km) from the city of Cairo in northern Egypt. Having endured more than 4,500 years, it is a lasting monument to the achievements of ancient Egyptian civilization. It was considered one of the Seven Wonders of the Ancient World. These were structures built in ancient times that were widely known and admired as remarkable achievements. The Great Pyramid is the only one still standing.

The Great Pyramid is also known as the pyramid of Khufu (KOO-foo), after the Egyptian king who had it built. It took more than 20 years to build the Great Pyramid. Construction began soon after Khufu, the son of Snefru, came to the throne around 2589 B.C. It was finished around the time he died in 2566 B.C.

More than 2,300,000 blocks of stone were used to build the Great Pyramid. Some of the limestone and granite blocks came from quarries 500 miles (805 km) away. The average weight of each stone is 2.5 tons (2.27 t, which means 2.27 metric tons), but some weigh as much as 9 tons (8.16 t). A few stones used in 1 of the chambers inside the pyramid weigh 60 tons (54.42 t). Altogether, the pyramid weighs 6.5 million tons (5.9 million t)! The stones were moved and put into place entirely through human effort, without the aid of wheels or machines.

The Great Pyramid (far right) is shown with the later pyramids of Khafre and Menkaure. The position from which the photograph below was taken makes it appear that Khafre's pyramid is tallest, but the Great Pyramid is actually tallest.

pyramid of Khafre

Great Pyramid

pyramid of Menkaure

Measuring the Exterior of the Great Pyramid

The Great Pyramid was the tallest building in the world for about 4,400 years. It was about 481 feet (about 160.33 yards) tall when it was completed. Over the centuries, the outer **casing** of stones disappeared from the pyramid. They were probably removed for use in other building projects. As a result, the pyramid is now only about 450 feet tall. What is the current height of the Great Pyramid in yards? To find the answer, divide the pyramid's height in feet by the number of feet in 1 yard (3 feet).

Current height in yards:

$$3)\overline{450} = 150 \text{ yards}$$

The current height of the Great Pyramid is 150 yards.

How would we find the current height in meters? A yard equals 0.9144 meter. To convert the height of the Great Pyramid from yards to meters, simply multiply the height in yards by the **conversion factor** of 0.9144. Round your answer to the nearest meter.

$$
\begin{array}{r}
0.9144 \\
\times\quad 150 \text{ yards} \\
\hline
0000 \\
45\,720 \\
+\ 91\,44 \\
\hline
137.1600 \text{ meters}
\end{array}
$$

The Great Pyramid is about 137 meters tall.

The **base** of the Great Pyramid is a square. Each side is about 756 feet long. How long is each side in yards? In meters?

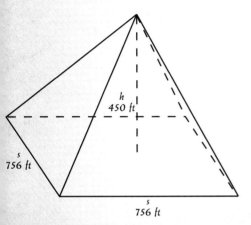

$$\frac{252 \text{ yards}}{3)\overline{756}}$$

$$\begin{array}{r} 0.9144 \\ \times \quad 252 \text{ yards} \\ \hline 1\,8288 \\ 45\,720 \\ +\,182\,88 \\ \hline 230.4288 \text{ meters} \end{array}$$

Each side of the base of the Great Pyramid is 252 yards or about 230 meters long.

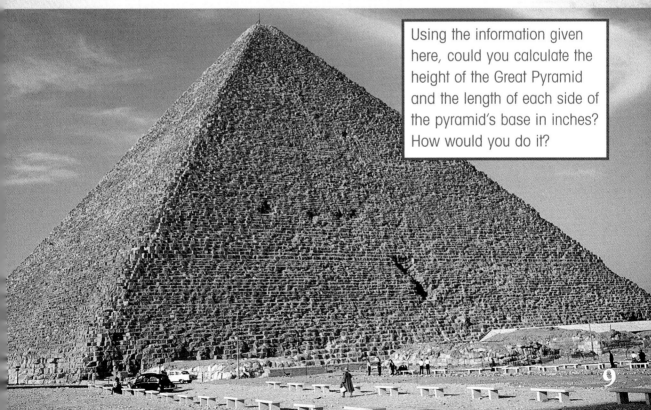

Using the information given here, could you calculate the height of the Great Pyramid and the length of each side of the pyramid's base in inches? How would you do it?

Now that we know the height of the Great Pyramid and the length of the sides of its base, let's figure out the total **surface area**. We'll start with the area of the base *(B)*. The base is a square, and the area of a square equals the square of the length of 1 side. This is the same as saying the area equals the length of the side times the length of the side. This is usually written as the formula: $A = s^2$. Since we've used *B* to represent the area of the base, we can write it as $B = s^2$. Remember that the area measurement is given in square units.

The formula $B = s^2$ can also be written B = s x s. This means that for the base of the Great Pyramid, B = 756 x 756.

$$
\begin{array}{r}
756 \text{ feet} \\
\times\ 756 \text{ feet} \\
\hline
4\,536 \\
37\,80 \\
+\ 529\,2 \\
\hline
571{,}536 \text{ square feet}
\end{array}
$$

The base of the Great Pyramid has an area of 571,536 square feet.

Next, let's find the area of 1 of the sloping triangular sides, or faces, of the Great Pyramid. To do this, we need to know the length of the base and the height of the face. In this case, the base of the triangle is 1 side of the square base of the pyramid. We've called it *s*, and we know *s* = 756 feet.

The height of 1 of the triangular sides is not the same as the height of the pyramid. Look at the diagram. The height of the Great Pyramid is measured by a line drawn straight down from the pyramid's **vertex** to a point on the pyramid's base directly below it. This line is **perpendicular** to the base of the pyramid. It's the line labeled *h* in the diagram. Now look at the line labeled *l*. This is the height of 1 of the faces, which is known as the slant height. It is a sloping line that runs along a face from the vertex to 1 side of the pyramid's base. Because the faces slope, this distance is greater than the distance from the vertex to the point on the base directly below it, and *l* is greater than *h*. The height *l* is 588 feet.

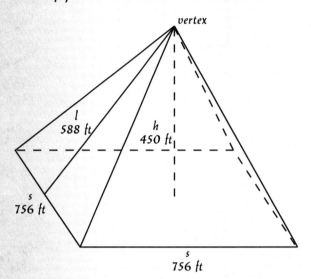

To understand why *l* is greater than *h*, it might help to imagine one of the pyramid's sides standing straight up, as shown in this diagram. Here, it's easy to see that *l* is greater than *h*.

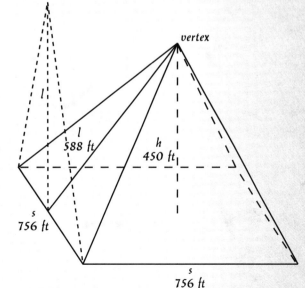

Now that we know the length of the base and the height for the sloping triangular faces of the Great Pyramid, we can calculate the area of a face. The area of a triangle equals $\frac{1}{2}$ the base times the height. This is usually written as the formula $A = \frac{1}{2}bh$, where b equals the base and h equals the height. Since we have already labeled the base s and the height l, we can write the formula $A = \frac{1}{2}sl$.

To find the area of 1 face of the Great Pyramid, multiply the base by the height and divide by 2.	756 feet x 588 feet 6 048 60 48 + 378 0 444,528 square feet	222,264 square feet 2)444,528

One face of the Great Pyramid has an area of 222,264 square feet.

We're finally ready to figure out the total surface area of the Great Pyramid. First, we need to multiply the area of 1 face by 4 to get the surface area of all 4 faces. Then, we add that product to the area of the pyramid base. The sum is the pyramid's total surface area.

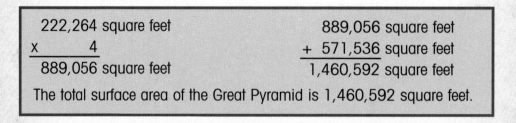

222,264 square feet x 4 889,056 square feet	889,056 square feet + 571,536 square feet 1,460,592 square feet

The total surface area of the Great Pyramid is 1,460,592 square feet.

What if we wanted to give the surface area in square yards? There are 9 square feet in 1 square yard, so we would divide the number of square feet by 9 to get the number of square yards.

$$\frac{162{,}288 \text{ square yards}}{9\overline{)1{,}460{,}592}}$$

The total surface area of the Great Pyramid is 162,288 square yards.

What if we wanted to give the surface area in square meters? A square yard equals 0.836 square meter. To convert the surface area to square meters, multiply the surface area in square yards by the conversion factor of 0.836.

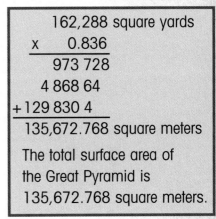

162,288 square yards
x   0.836
973 728
4 868 64
+129 830 4
135,672.768 square meters

The total surface area of the Great Pyramid is 135,672.768 square meters.

This photograph shows the Great Pyramid from above, surrounded by smaller pyramids and other structures. These were temples and burial places for royal relatives and officials.

The Interior of the Great Pyramid

Unlike modern buildings, the Great Pyramid does not have lots of open space inside. In fact, it is almost solid stone! Try to imagine what that means for such a huge structure. Remember, the pyramid is 450 feet (137 m) tall, and each side of its base is 756 feet (230 m) long. Think of that enormous interior almost completely filled with stone. That's why it took more than 2,300,000 blocks of stone to build the Great Pyramid, and that's why the pyramid weighs 6.5 million tons (5.9 million t).

Let's calculate the volume of the Great Pyramid. Volume is measured in cubic units. A cubic foot, for example, is a cube whose height, width, and depth are each 1 foot. A cubic yard is a cube whose height, width, and depth are each 1 yard.

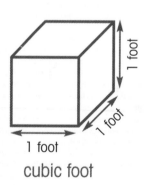

1 foot

1 foot

1 foot

cubic foot

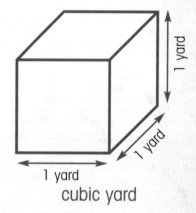

1 yard

1 yard

1 yard

cubic yard

The volume of a pyramid equals $\frac{1}{3}$ the area of the base times the height. We can write this as the formula $V = (\frac{1}{3})Bh$. (B = the area of the base and h = height.) We know the height of the Great Pyramid—450 feet—and we've already calculated the area of the base: 571,536 square feet.

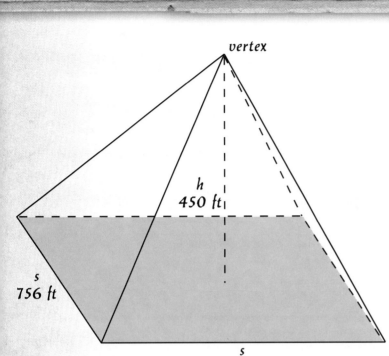

vertex

h
450 ft

s
756 ft

s
756 ft

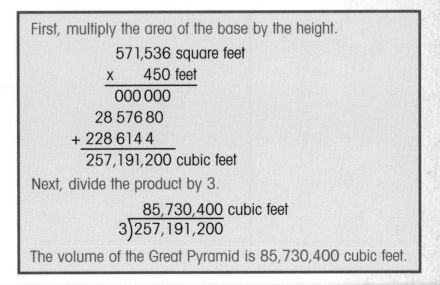

First, multiply the area of the base by the height.

571,536 square feet
x   450 feet
_____
000 000
28 576 80
+ 228 614 4
_____
257,191,200 cubic feet

Next, divide the product by 3.

85,730,400 cubic feet
3)257,191,200

The volume of the Great Pyramid is 85,730,400 cubic feet.

What is the volume of the Great Pyramid in cubic yards? First, we need to know how many cubic feet are in 1 cubic yard. Since 1 yard equals 3 feet, a cubic yard is a cube that is 3 feet by 3 feet by 3 feet.

That means there are 27 cubic feet in 1 cubic yard. Divide the number of cubic feet in the Great Pyramid by 27 to get the number of cubic yards.

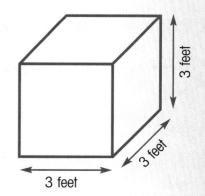

3 feet

3 feet

3 feet

```
           3,175,200 cubic yards
      27) 85,730,400
          – 81
          ─────
           47
          – 27
          ─────
           203
          – 189
          ─────
           140
          – 135
          ─────
            54
          – 54
          ─────
            000
```

The volume of the Great Pyramid is 3,175,200 cubic yards.

Some say that there are enough stones in the Great Pyramid to build a wall 10 feet (3 m) high and 1 foot (0.3 m) thick all the way around France!

If we want to give the volume of the Great Pyramid in cubic meters, we would multiply the number of cubic yards by a conversion factor of 0.765, since 1 cubic yard equals 0.765 cubic meter.

```
        3,175,200 cubic yards    The volume of the Great Pyramid
     x        0.765              is 2,429,028 cubic meters.
        15 876 000
       190 512 00
   + 2222 6400
     2,429,028.000 cubic meters
```

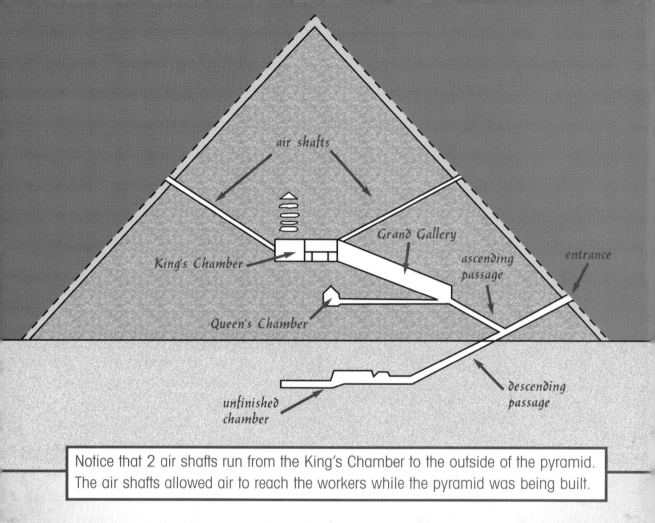

air shafts

Grand Gallery

King's Chamber

ascending passage

entrance

Queen's Chamber

unfinished chamber

descending passage

Notice that 2 air shafts run from the King's Chamber to the outside of the pyramid. The air shafts allowed air to reach the workers while the pyramid was being built.

The Great Pyramid is not completely solid. Inside are 2 rooms with passages leading to them. The large room known as the King's Chamber may be where King Khufu was buried. However, some people believe he was buried in a room below the pyramid. The small room is known as the Queen's Chamber. It was probably originally intended to be Khufu's burial chamber, but then the plans were changed.

Workers needed a way to get inside the pyramid while it was being built. The entrance, which was concealed after the pyramid was completed, is located on the north face about 50 feet (15 m) above the base. A short, narrow descending passage leads down from the entrance. About 95 feet (29 m) from the entrance, a cramped ascending passage starts upward from the descending passage. The ascending passage is about 125 feet (38 m) long. At the end of it are 2 other passages. A narrow **horizontal** passage about 125 feet (38 m) long leads to the Queen's Chamber. The other passage, about 157 feet (48 m) long, is a large ascending hallway known as the Grand Gallery. It leads to the King's Chamber. Directly above the King's Chamber, but not connected to it, are several small, empty chambers. **Archaeologists** believe these empty spaces were meant to reduce the amount of weight pressing down on the King's Chamber so the chamber's roof would not collapse. The weight of the stones used in the chamber's roof was already considerable without the weight of the stones above it. Builders lined the King's Chamber with blocks of granite. The massive blocks used in the ceiling weigh as much as 60 tons (54.42 t) each.

The King's Chamber is about 17 feet wide, 34 feet long, and 19 feet tall. What is its volume?

First, multiply the length by the width.	34 feet x 17 feet 238 + 34 578 square feet	Then, multiply that product by the height.	578 square feet x 19 feet 5 202 + 578 10,982 cubic feet

The volume of the King's Chamber is 10,982 cubic feet.

What is the volume of the King's Chamber in cubic yards? Divide the volume in cubic feet by 27 to get the number of cubic yards. Round to the nearest whole number.

```
            406.7 cubic yards
     27) 10,982.0
        - 108
            18
          - 0
           182
          -162
            200
           -189
            11
```

The volume of the King's Chamber is about 407 cubic yards.

What is the approximate volume of the King's Chamber in cubic meters? Multiply the number of cubic yards by the conversion factor of 0.765. Round your answer to the nearest whole number.

```
    407 cubic yards
  x 0.765
    2 035
   24 42
 + 284 9
  311.355 cubic meters
```

The volume of the King's Chamber is about 311 cubic meters.

This painting shows what an artist imagined the King's Chamber looked like when Arab explorers entered it in A.D. 820.

The Queen's Chamber is about 17 feet wide, 19 feet long, and 20 feet tall. How would you find its volume in cubic feet? How would you find its volume in cubic yards? How would you find its volume in cubic meters?

Measuring the Angles of the Great Pyramid

The sloping faces of a pyramid determine how it looks. Faces with a steep slope make tall, narrow pyramids. Faces with a gradual slope make low, broad pyramids. A tall, narrow pyramid would have been too difficult for the ancient Egyptians to build. A low, broad pyramid would not have been impressive enough for the tomb of a king. The ancient Egyptians chose to build something between those 2 designs. Let's measure the slope of the Great Pyramid's faces. This is the same as measuring the angles formed where the faces meet the pyramid's base. First, let's review some basic points about angles.

- When 2 planes **intersect**, a line is formed. When 3 planes intersect, an angle is formed.
- Angles are measured in degrees.
- Angles can be measured with a tool called a protractor.
- The size of an angle is not affected by the length of the angle's sides.
- The measurements of the 3 angles of a triangle always add up to 180°.

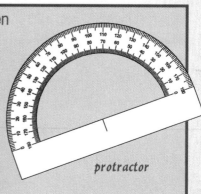

protractor

Now let's measure the slope of the Great Pyramid's faces. Study the picture here, which shows a protractor placed over a simple drawing of the Great Pyramid. The slope or angle is about 51°. Use your own protractor to measure the slope or angle of the opposite side. You should find that it's also about 51°.

What is the angle of the Great Pyramid's vertex? You can measure it with your protractor, but there's another way to find it. Since the 3 angles of a triangle always add up to 180°, you can add the measurements of the 2 angles we know and subtract that sum from 180°. The difference will equal the vertex. Try both methods and see what you get. You should find that the vertex is about 78°.

Now use your protractor to measure the slope or angle of the descending passage inside the Great Pyramid. What do you get? You should find the angle of the descending passage to be about 26°. Next, use your protractor to measure the slope or angle of the ascending passage. What do you get? You should find that the angle of the ascending passage is about the same as that of the descending passage.

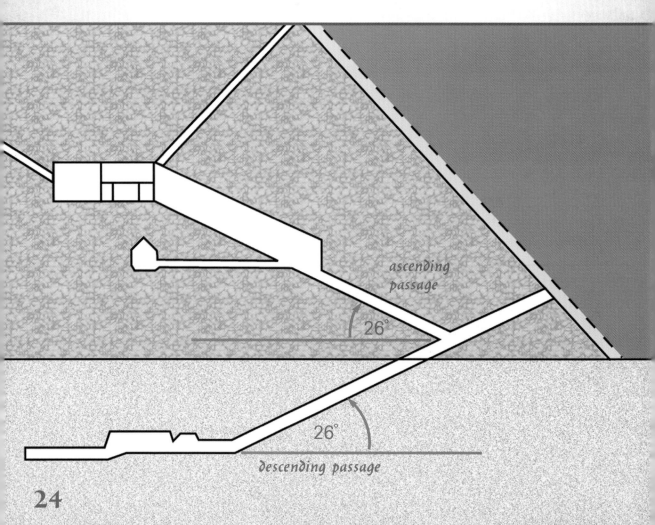

ascending passage

26°

26°

descending passage

There's a reason the ancient Egyptians made these passages sloping instead of flat. Gold, furniture, and other costly objects were buried with the king for his *ka* to use in the afterlife. Thieves knew about the riches in the pyramids and wanted to steal them. The builders used sloping instead of flat passages to make it harder for thieves to succeed.

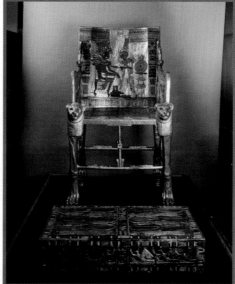

These objects came from the tomb of King Tutankhamen, who died around 1325 B.C. Similar objects would have been buried with King Khufu, though none were found in the Great Pyramid. Most people believe Khufu's burial objects were stolen by thieves long ago.

The Pyramids of Khafre and Menkaure

Near the Great Pyramid are 2 other enormous pyramids. One was built by Khufu's son Khafre (KAF-ray). The other was built by Khafre's son Menkaure (men-KOW-ray). Let's take a look at them and see what we can learn using the math skills we've been practicing.

Khafre's pyramid was begun around 2558 B.C. and finished around 2532 B.C. It is almost—but not quite—as large as the Great Pyramid. It was originally about 471 feet (144 m) tall; today it is about 446 feet (136 m) tall. The slant height of each face is about 568 feet (173 m). Each side of the base is about 704 feet (215 m) long. The slope or angle of each face is about 53°. Khafre's pyramid is solid stone. There are no rooms inside. The burial chamber is below it.

What is the height of Khafre's pyramid in yards? What is its height in meters? What is the length of 1 side in yards? What is the length in meters? If you need help finding the answers to these questions, review the information on pages 8 and 9.

What is the total surface area of Khafre's pyramid? Do you know how to find it? If you need help, review the information on pages 10 through 13.

Khafre's pyramid is the only one that still has some of the brilliant white limestone casing stones in place. You can see them near the pyramid's vertex.

Menkaure's pyramid was built sometime during his reign, which lasted from about 2490 B.C. until about 2472 B.C. It is by far the smallest of the 3 large pyramids. It was originally about 215 feet (66 m) tall; today it is about 203 feet (62 m) tall. The slant height of each face is about 266 feet (81 m). Each side of the base is about 344 feet (105 m) long. The slope or angle of each face is about 51°. Like Khafre's pyramid, it is solid stone. The burial chamber is beneath it.

What is the length of 1 side in yards? What is the length in meters? What is the area of the base? What is the area of 1 face?

What is the volume of Menkaure's pyramid in cubic feet? Do you know how to find it? If you need help, review the information on pages 14 and 15. What is the volume in cubic yards? What is the volume in cubic meters? If you need help, review the information on pages 16 and 17.

What is the angle of the vertex of Menkaure's pyramid? If you need help, review the information on pages 22 and 23.

Menkaure's pyramid was covered with white limestone casing on the top and red granite casing on the bottom. It is said that Menkaure planned to cover the entire surface of the pyramid with granite but died before he was able to complete it.

"Time Fears the Pyramids"

"Man fears Time, yet Time fears the pyramids." This Arab **proverb** expresses the awe and wonder the pyramids inspire. They were built by a civilization that did not have wheels or machines, yet the pyramids have survived for 4,500 years. Archaeologists still argue about exactly how they were built, and we may never know.

However, the pyramids show us that the ancient Egyptians had remarkable math skills. Each corner of the pyramids' bases is an almost perfect right angle. The workers were able to make such precise measurements that the sides of each pyramid's base are the same length. The faces of each pyramid have the same angle or slope. The stones were cut so exactly that they fit together with almost no space between them. The more we study the pyramids, the more we can see the important role that math played in constructing them. Who knows—if you continue to develop your math skills, you might one day build something that will last as long as the pyramids and will inspire wonder for thousands of years!

Glossary

afterlife (AF-tuhr-lyf) The life of the spirit after death.

archaeologist (ahr-kee-AH-luh-jist) A scientist who studies ancient buildings and objects to learn how people lived in the past.

base (BAYS) The bottom of a pyramid or the lower edge of a triangle.

casing (KAY-sing) An outer layer or covering.

conversion factor (kuhn-VUHR-zhun FAK-tuhr) A number by which you multiply or divide to convert between different units of measurement.

horizontal (hohr-uh-ZAHN-tuhl) Parallel to the horizon or to a baseline.

intersect (in-tuhr-SEKT) To meet and cross.

perpendicular (puhr-puhn-DIH-kyuh-luhr) Meeting at right angles.

proverb (PRAH-vuhrb) A short saying that expresses a commonly accepted idea or truth.

surface area (SUHR-fuhs EHR-ee-uh) The area of the entire surface of a 3-dimensional form.

vertex (VUHR-teks) The point where the sides of an angle meet or the top of a pyramid.

Index